Get the digital guide:
mural.co/ebook

The Definitive Guide To Facilitating Remote Workshops

Authors: Mark Tippin, Jim Kalbach, David Chin

Second Edition: June 2019

Everyone in the business of creating or improving something is designing.

All change starts with a vision and requires hustle, so we like to call change-makers Imagination Workers. And when Imagination Workers with different skill sets and backgrounds team up together - big ideas come to life.

Our mission at MURAL is to inspire, enhance, and connect Imagination Workers globally.

We believe that innovation, change, can happen anywhere, as long as great minds can be connected and collaborate towards a common goal.

For global teams, MURAL is the space where that magic happens.

So here is our contribution to accelerate your transformation and your organization's.

In the next few pages, you'll find a condensed version of suggestions, best practices, and stories from the trenches to guide you to become the best facilitator of Imagination Workers.

Mariano Suarez-Battan
CEO @ MURAL

CONT

ENTS

PART I

DIGITAL-FIRST MINDSET

Everything we know about work is changing: where it's done, how it's done and who does it.

Most conversations are not going to be face to face, and we need courageous facilitators to broker dialogues between a widening range of stakeholders.

As facilitators, we work to create conditions where vital dialogues flourish. We've all come to wield an astonishingly clever range of tools and materials to unleash team potential. But as the circumstances of work evolve, so too must our mastery of new venues for facilitation. Where these lessons happen is the focus of this book. We aim to show you how, with forethought, conducting remote workshops can be as productive as running them in person.

How? By going digital first.

This requires a mindset shift. Make digital collaboration your starting point, not an afterthought. This takes practice and patience, as **Doug Powell**, Distinguished Designer at IBM, told us: **"Changing team behavior doesn't happen in a single meeting. Give it some time. Learn and adapt."**

Solving creative problems isn't the same as facilitating groups who are solving creative problems. This is true for disciplines like engineering and product management as well. Getting others to actively participate in the conversation requires talented, enthusiastic facilitators. We must look beyond the limits of the room to involve key voices in the discussion - no matter where they are located.

It's taken us hundreds of remote sessions with scores of dispersed teams to tease out what works best in remote workshops. In one case we ran three experiments with **Jeff Gothelf**, the author of *Lean UX*, just to focus on making his curriculum remote-friendly. In turn, those insights helped FanDuel build products while working across multiple continents.

(Read about the FanDuel case at http://mur.al/leanux)

When we surveyed our collective experiences we were able to identify three key considerations that underpin all effective remote workshops:

TEAMS: Teams have a shape, and your strategy needs to take that into account.

TOOLS: Get agreement on the essential technologies.

TECHNIQUES: Rethink your methods to be remote-friendly.

With these factors sorted, you're ready to clearly define the team's target outcome and work towards that objective.

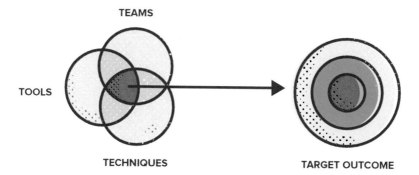

TEAMS

TOOLS

TECHNIQUES

TARGET OUTCOME

This book assumes that the reader has some experience developing and delivering workshops. However, if you have no facilitation experience you will still find this book helpful. In the end, remote collaboration is a group activity. This book is also instructional for remote workshop participants desiring to improve their interactions.

Your teams are moving into a future filled with remote collaboration, and everyone has a role in the success. Consider what **Rachel Smith***, facilitator with The Grove, told us: **"Remote facilitation is making it easier for people to do work without being in the same room they are in. Although there are professional facilitators, there are lots of ways to be facilitative that anyone on a remote team can employ."**

*The Grove Consultants International are leaders in graphic facilitation. They offer many tools and products for facilitation on their website, grove.com. Rachel Smith is an expert remote facilitator who excels at integrating technology into visual practice. She blogs at digitalfacilitation.net.

The way team members are organized affects how they'll interact.

Team shape is defined by the location of individual members. While co-located teams are still common, it's rare to find a team that NEVER works with at least one remote participant. Here are the three team configurations you'll most likely encounter:

SPLIT TEAMS
Two or more co-located teams collaborate between defined locations

HYBRID TEAMS
One co-located team collaborates with remote participants

REMOTE TEAMS
No central location, everyone is 100% remote

Our research shows that hybrid teams are the most common configuration (with remote teams in second place). The challenge with hybrid teams is that they tend to exclude remote colleagues. Facilitators must work to involve everyone. As **Dave Malouf**, designer and founder of the IxDA, says: **"If one person is not in the room, no one is in the room."**

Strategize for the different team shapes you find. Ultimately, your goal is to create a balanced interaction and psychological safety so everyone can contribute.

TEAMS
PRO TIPS

GET A HEAD START
Use group chat to meet and communicate before the workshop. Send a survey to gather background information from participants to inform your planning.

ACKNOWLEDGE DIFFERENCES
Recognize the different contexts and have participants describe their environment (location, time, workspace) to build team rapport.

DIRECT TRAFFIC
Turn-taking is more difficult in remote settings. Call on participants one at a time. Use a list of attendees or have each person nominate the next one to share out.

DIVIDE IN ADVANCE
Give thought to dividing workshop participants into breakout groups or smaller teams ahead of time. Avoid creating groups on-the-fly.

SHARE AND SHARE ALIKE
Post all workshop output in a common location as it's created.

DON'T LET CO-LOCATED GROUPS DOMINATE
Get everyone involved in the discussion, especially if they're not in the room. Leave space so others can jump in.

GO ALL REMOTE
Level the playing field by having everyone dial in, even if some of the team are in the same office building.

TEAMS
KEY QUESTIONS

HOW MANY PEOPLE WILL PARTICIPATE?
The number of participants impacts how you coordinate interactions, e.g., group discussion vs breakout groups.

HOW DISPERSED IS THE GROUP?
Consider how distance plays a role in interaction. Sometimes a participant's level of remoteness from others becomes a disadvantage.

WHAT ARE THE TIME ZONE DIFFERENCES?
Be aware of times, dates, and holidays when scheduling a session. As one participant is just waking up, another may be winding down.

WHO CAN HELP FACILITATE?
Don't run remote workshops alone. Enlist others as co-facilitators, discussion leads, and scribes. Assign roles in advance.

WHAT CAN BE ACCOMPLISHED ASYNCHRONOUSLY?
Maximize together time and push some activities to before and after the workshop.

Not another tool!

We hear that all time. While tool fatigue is all too common, remote workshops rely on applications to make the interaction possible. Choose tools you'll use based on five key capabilities needed for remote workshops:

Think Visually
sharing assets with digital whiteboards

Share Content
with online documents and shared drives

Stay Organized
with calendars and project tracking systems

Communicate In Real-Time
with video conferencing

Communicate Asynchronously
with email and chat

FIVE KEY CAPABILITIES NEEDED FOR REMOTE WORKSHOPS

COMMUNICATE IN REAL-TIME	See everyone's smile and hear everyone's voice when you meet.	**Recommended:** Zoom **Alternative:** Skype, Bluejeans
COMMUNICATE ASYNCHRONOUSLY	Create a community before you meet and stay connected between sessions.	**Recommended:** Slack **Alternative:** SMS, HipChat
SHARE CONTENT	Establish the location where videos, PDFs, and other necessary files are stored.	**Recommended:** Google Drive **Alternative:** Dropbox, Box
STAY ORGANIZED	Track resources, events, and assignments to keep the team aligned.	**Recommended:** Trello **Alternative:** Asana, BaseCamp
THINK VISUALLY	Collaborate, brainstorm, share artifacts and interact like you're in the same room.	**Recommended:** MURAL **Complementary:** UxPin, Invision

As the facilitator, you should be comfortable with each tool used in the workshop. Be able to guide others on their use and troubleshoot issues. As **Dave Gray***, author and founder of XPLANE, advises: **"Keep it simple. Practice the tech beforehand. Test it on people who have not used the software before to identify possible fail points."**

Use multiple channels to engage participants. Create a flow that changes mode of interaction to hold their attention.

I'D RATHER HAVE A
GREAT TEAM WITH BAD TOOLS
than a bad team with great tools.

The great team will find ways to communicate well, regardless of the tools.

SCOTT BERKUN / Author & Speaker, Berkun Media

*Dave Gray is an author of "Gamestorming" and founder of XPLANE, the visual thinking company. He helps people develop shared understanding, so they can make better, faster decisions, and work better together to create more lasting, sustainable impact. For more, see http://www.xplane.com

Scott Berkun (scottberkun.com) is a well-known author and speaker who is active in understanding remote work. His book, A Year Without Pants, recounts his stint at Automattic, a 100% remote company.

PRO TIPS

BRING YOUR OWN DEVICE (BYOD)
Log into the workshop with multiple devices to share visuals via webcams. Have mobile phones handy for photos.

ORIENT TO TOOLS
Review the tools and their functions with the whole group at the beginning. Troubleshoot with the help of a co-facilitator as needed.

PRACTICE SWITCHING CHANNELS
Get the whole team used to moving fluidly between tools: from video conferencing to chats to documents and back, for instance.

SET UP RELIABLE AUDIO
Bad audio is a showstopper. Set up clear audio channels with good mics.

TURN ON WEBCAMS
Use webcams for nonverbal communication, e.g., thumbs-up for an OK or hand raise to vote. Keep them close up to see facial expressions as well.

VISUALIZE THE ACTION
Use an online whiteboard, like MURAL, to support visual thinking and sharing photos of sketches and flipcharts.

HAVE A PLAN B
Technology fails. Have fall-back communication channels and alternatives.

TOOLS
KEY QUESTIONS

DOES EVERYONE HAVE ACCESS?
Make sure everyone has the necessary applications installed or online accounts ready well in advance.

DOES EVERYONE KNOW HOW TO USE THE TOOLS?
Practice using the tools. Onboard everyone with warm-up exercise that requires participants to use each one.

WHICH TOOLS ARE CRITICAL FOR THE INTERACTION?
Run through the interactions you're planning in order to troubleshoot any logistical issues beforehand.

HOW DO THE TOOLS WORK WITH EACH OTHER?
Think about which tool is best for each exercise. Assign each tool a function for consistency.

HOW WILL YOU INTEGRATE INFORMATION AFTERWARDS?
Consider what needs to happen with the content after the workshop and set up documents in advance.

The effectiveness of your next remote workshop will depend on the techniques you'll include and the manner in which you implement them.

Don't assume that a technique you ran yesterday in a room full of people will work the same way tomorrow in an online collaboration. Passing sketches from one table to another or performing a "gallery crawl" becomes a challenge when the physical space is removed. Review each activity, understand its intent, and then transform it into a remote-friendly technique as needed.

In-person workshops have a predictable format; half-day, full-day or multi-day. Why? Because there is a large investment in time and travel cost, so you pack in a lot of action to get the ROI. But does this have to be the case for remote workshops?

Consider how you might flip these three aspects around for surprising results:

Synchronous vs. Asynchronous Participation: Remote workshops are more flexible than in-person sessions. How might you spread the workshop out over time? Try scheduling multiple "power hours" with time in between to tie up loose ends and prepare for the next wave.

Individual vs. Group Activity: Even when the video conference tool supports it, creating breakout groups online is less fluid than it is in person. Explore ways to reach a similar outcome leveraging more individual work followed by share-outs to the whole team.

Verbal vs. Non-Verbal Collaboration: Much of the nonverbal communication goes away in remote workshops. How can you fill the gap? Use webcams to get a "thumbs-up" from everyone or see heads nodding in agreement. Emojis and GIFs in chats can enhance nonverbal communication too.

A digital-first mindset involves more than choosing tools: it's a new way of thinking about methods. **Dom Price**, Head of R&D and futurist at Atlassian puts it this way: "**Before you try any products, make sure you get your practices right. If you don't understand how you want to work with someone, no tool will solve that.**"

When trying to employ a traditional method in a virtual session, look at the objective, and then be creative in how to get the same results with digital tools. In some cases, the digital-first results can even provide better results than their traditional predecessors.

RE-IMAGINE TRADITIONAL METHODS FOR ONLINE

TRADITIONAL METHOD	METHOD OBJECTIVE	DIGITAL-FIRST ALTERNATIVE	DIGITAL ADVANTAGE
Warm-up exercise asking table groups to find three things they all have in common.	Get people to learn something new about each other.	Have everyone describe themselves with photos in MURAL.	Sharing photos makes the experience more personal.
Brainstorming with sticky notes.	Get lots of ideas externalized.	Have everyone brainstorm ideas in a pre-workshop MURAL, then cluster and discuss.	Working asynchronously - in advance - allows the team to use their time more efficiently. Being able to brainstorm when you're in the mood rather than on demand can lead to higher quality ideas.
Voting with colored sticky dots to show the solution each person likes most.	Visualize the preferences among the participants in the workshop.	Use a poll, or the built-in voting functionality in MURAL.	MURAL's built-in voting functionality speeds up the process and allows for additional rounds of voting. Results from multiple voting sessions can be quickly reviewed so everyone can clearly see how preferences changed over time.
Break into groups to sketch out a concept poster to pitch your solution.	Create an artifact that distills your idea, value proposition and action plan.	Use Zoom's breakout rooms to place people into groups and LUMA Institute's templates in MURAL to prepare a work area in advance.	MURAL makes it easy to build compelling visuals, Zoom connects participants into groups. LUMA templates make it quick to prepare workshops.

To get you jump started, we've included a range of remote-ready workshop methods in part two of the book, "Digital-First Practice."

TECHNIQUES
PRO TIPS

CREATE A WORKSHOP DASHBOARD
Keep multiple parts of your workshop in one place, like a virtual canvas, so you can see the bigger picture.

REHEARSE
Run through your exercises to "de-bug" the logistics. Make sure participants have clear instructions by trying them out yourself.

TIMEBOX EVERYTHING
Break down your methods into small chunks (5-10 minutes) and set the timer to keep the process focused.

EXPLOIT MULTITASKING
Integrate remote participants' ability to multitask by giving impromptu tasks, like searching for examples.

SOLICIT FEEDBACK
Make the session interactive by using polls, voting and dialogue tools to engage participants.

DIGITIZE AS YOU GO
For participants working face-to-face, don't wait to convert physical artifacts to a digital format – do it as you create them.

WORK ASYNCHRONOUSLY
Plan activities to be completed before and after workshops, e.g., have participants collect data or examples ahead of time.

DON'T STOP AT THE END
Keep iterating on your own time and encourage others to do the same.

TECHNIQUES
KEY QUESTIONS

WHAT ARE THE DESIRED OUTCOMES?
Make sure the team is clear about the objectives in order to keep everyone on track.

WHAT'S THE EXPECTED DELIVERABLE?
To make sharing and distribution simple, results will need to be digital. Prepare target documents to gather team output.

HOW CAN EXERCISES BE DIVIDED UP?
Break down activities into shorter exercises (e.g., 5-10 minutes each) to minimize the risk of getting off track.

WHAT'S YOUR PLAN B?
Have a backup plan if you have technical difficulties or your activity gets derailed.

HOW CAN PEOPLE FOLLOW UP?
Set up management tools in advance to assign owners and follow-up tasks, and to track ongoing progress.

ESSENTIAL FACTORS

TIME ZONES

Strive to schedule workshops during working hours for all participants. The further away time zones are, the shorter the overlapping window.

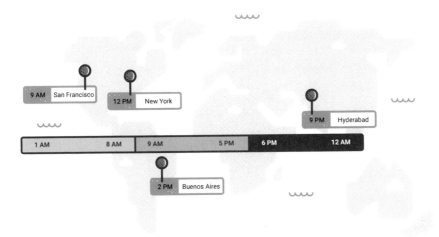

For example, if you want to run a workshop between Team 1 on the West Coast of the US and Team 2 on the East Coast, you'll have five hours of overlap. Throw in Team 3 in Buenos Aires, and the overlap drops to only three hours between all three locations.

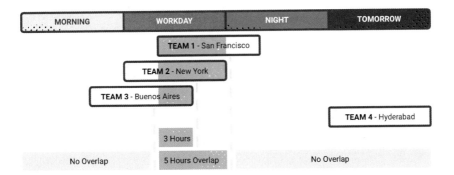

Add in Hyderabad, and there is NO overlap. In this case, some participants will have to join outside working hours. And if your team spans the international date line, the workshop might be on different days. A Thursday workshop in Denver falls on Friday in Shanghai.

Arrange off-hours workshops well in advance and make sure participants approve. Study the participant list and make sure all folks are essential, particularly if you're requesting people join after business hours.

"I have noticed that having high-contrast cultures can tire out the group a little more," observes **Lee Duncan**, UX Designer at IBM. **"For this reason, I have a bias toward energetic hours, smaller groups (or localized geo-asyncing) and again carefully consider the level of culture contrast."**

Time zones present a big challenge for many dispersed teams. Even **John Maeda**, design thought leader and author of numerous books, recognizes the impact: **"When working with a completely remote team, maintaining empathy for time zone differences is key."**

Don't get caught with your guard down. Consider these tips for working across time zones:

Use a Time Zone Calculator: There are a range of services to help figure time zones out, such as World Time Buddy (www.worldtimebuddy.com).

Schedule Multiple Sessions: Split the workshop into multiple, smaller sections.

Enlist a Distant Co-Facilitator: Hire co-facilitators in another time zone.

Work Asynchronously: Assign pre- and post-work to reduce time zone strain.

Rotate Early or Late Shifts: Alternate which team will be inconvenienced.

Avoid Monday and Friday: Don't make one group work into the weekend.

Consider Holidays: Holiday schedules are different across countries.

Be Aware of Summer Time: Not all countries switch or do so on different dates. Also remember inverted seasons between Northern and Southern hemispheres.

Respect Different Meal Times: Customary meal times differ from country to country. For instance, in Argentina people eat lunch and dinner later than they do in the US.

AUDIO

With any remote interaction, you have to get the technology right. Don't skimp on audio or video—they're critical.

Bad audio is a showstopper. Test in advance and consider a backup plan, e.g., have direct phone numbers to call. Here are the four main concerns with audio when running remote workshops:

CHOOSE THE BEST AUDIO OPTION

There are three means to connect audio:

- Wired telephones and speaker phones provide the most reliable audio connection. Use them for co-located groups and dedicated remote workers whenever possible.

- Cellular telephones have a dedicated connection that is separate from the wifi you may be using. You can often improve your experience by taking advantage of both cellular service for audio and wifi for screen sharing and video.

- Voice-over IP (VoIP) refers to digitized audio streaming through your computer, commonly found in programs like Skype, Lync or Viber. Audio quality suffers when wifi bandwidth is limited, the connection is poor, or there is high demand for available bandwidth. Turn off webcams to free up bandwidth, and use a hard-wired ethernet connection for better performance, if possible.

OPTIMIZE MICROPHONES

There are two common microphone types:

- Cardioid mics focus their attention on what is in front of them.

- Omni-directional mics can pick up sound from any direction.

If you're dialing in from remote locations, get a quality, wired headset with a cardioid condenser mic. If you're part of a co-located team, get a quality speakerphone with an omnidirectional mic so everyone can speak and hear. USB omni-directional mics are also a good option if are using VOIP on a computer.

AVOID FEEDBACK

When a microphone gets too close to a speaker, what comes out of the speaker "feeds back" into the mic. This loop quickly becomes an annoying screech.

Imagine a video conference with five co-located members and five remote members. As long as the co-located team uses a single mic and speaker, things are fine. But when someone else in the same room joins the call, the audio from one device is picked up by the mic of another. This might also happen if a remote person connected to the call on a cell phone and computer. Either way, the result is feedback.

Prevent feedback by muting your phone or laptop before entering the call. Many conference services allow a host to mute everyone at once or individuals one at a time. If this isn't possible, have the presenter locate the live mic and then ask everyone else to mute.

ELIMINATE ECHO

Echo makes it impossible to participate in a meeting. If you're hearing the echo, the good news is that you're not causing the echo. The bad news is that the person causing the echo probably doesn't know there's a problem.

Echo primarily affects remote callers, but they are rarely the cause. This puts the burden on remote callers to stop the show and insist on diagnosing the problem. As a facilitator, you should help.

First, mute everyone who isn't talking. This should stop the echo, but the problem will return unless you diagnose it further:

- Ensure co-located groups are using only one microphone, all others are muted.

- Reduce speaker volume or move speakers further apart from each other.

- Check that remote people using a phone have their computers muted too.

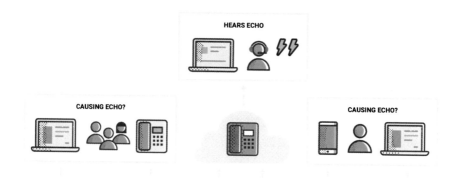

VIDEO

There are two things people need to see in a meeting. They need to see each other, and they need to see the content being discussed.

In co-located meetings it takes zero technology. Just look around to see everyone and everything. In a fully distributed workshop, this is also pretty easy. You connect to a video conference and share your screen.

But when some people are in a room together and some are remote, you'll need to put more effort into video.

This diagram shows the planning required for a mixed-location, interactive design workshop. One group is co-located in an auditorium while others connect from locations around the world. This type of "Mixed Team" setting requires an extreme amount of planning and coordination.

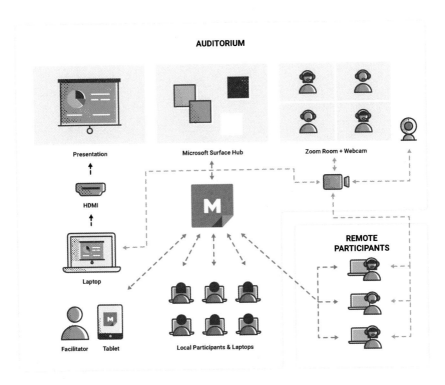

Local and remote participants need to see each other. Ensure webcams are zoomed in to see facial expressions. They must also have access to any presentation slides as well as the online workspace for collaborating.

It's the most challenging to execute well, but doing so prepares you for almost any situation you are likely to encounter.

IN CO-LOCATED WORKPLACES, PEOPLE OFTEN COMMUNICATE WITHOUT REALIZING IT.

Their body language, door position, and visible computer monitor says something about their workload and status.

When working remotely, you have to work extra hard, communicating these things often - whether via email, instant messenger, MURAL, or phone - in order to stay in sync with your team.

KAILEY HOWELL / Executive Creative Director, Fullscreen Media

Kailey and her creative team at Fullscreen are consummate remote workers. They think digital first in order to be inclusive of everyone on the team, regardless of where they are. Some of the earliest adopters of MURAL, Kailey's team regularly works on media campaigns that are highly visual in nature - all digital and all online.

GROUP SIZE

As a facilitator, your role is to ensure that workshop activities flow, and people stay engaged in the process.

One often-overlooked factor when planning a workshop is determining the optimum number of people to include. Workshops work well with 12, 16 or 24 people. Why? Because they provide the most flexibility when doing breakout sessions while including enough people to help the diversity of ideas and discussions.

Other important factors to consider when deciding the appropriate group size for your workshop are the following:

WORKSHOP LENGTH
The more people you include, the more time you'll need for introductions, sharing out and reflection. Twenty-four people in a one hour workshop won't allow for significant participation.

UNTESTED CONTENT
If you're running a workshop for the first time, consider doing a pilot with a smaller group to expose gaps and get feedback in order to improve the experience.

RACI
Responsible, Accountable, Consulted and Informed. Who needs to participate in the workshop? Who could just be informed of the outcomes afterwards? Who needs to leave with assignments?

DEMAND
If demand is high for your workshop, you may need to include more people per workshop than you'd prefer. Adjust your curriculum accordingly.

IDEAL RATIO
Complex topics with ambitious agendas have a better chance of success with fewer participants. Straightforward topics involving fewer exercises still flow with larger groups.

OPTIMAL GROUP SIZES

GROUP SIZE	BREAKOUT OPTIONS
6	2 Groups of 3 People 3 Groups of 2 People
8	2 Groups of 4 People 4 Groups of 2 People
10	2 Groups of 5 People 5 Groups of 2 People
12	2 Groups of 6 People **3 Groups of 4 People** **4 Groups of 3 People** **6 Groups of 2 People**
14	2 Groups of 7 People **7 Groups of 2 People**
15	**3 Groups of 5 People** **5 Groups of 3 People**
16	2 Groups of 8 People **4 Groups of 4 People** **8 Groups of 2 People**
18	3 Groups of 6 People **6 Groups of 3 People**
20	**4 Groups of 5 People** **5 Groups of 4 People**
21	3 Groups of 7 People **7 Groups of 3 People**
24	3 Groups of 8 People 4 Groups of 6 People **6 Groups of 4 People** **8 Groups of 3 People**

This chart shows the breakout options available for the most common group sizes.

Bold text indicates optimum sizes for the breakout groups (2-5 people).

TIMING

A common mistake when designing a workshop is leaving too little time for groups to share out after they complete an activity.

This can destroy your timing and frustrate your participants to no end.

The chart below provides a quick reference for determining how much time is needed to hear share outs based on how much time you give per share.

		Time Allowed Per Share Out							
		15 Sec	30 Sec	60 Sec	90 Sec	2 Min	3 Min	4 Min	5 Min
	1	0:00:15	0:00:30	0:01:00	0:01:30	0:02:00	0:03:00	0:04:00	0:05:00
	2	0:00:30	0:01:00	0:02:00	0:03:00	0:04:00	0:06:00	0:08:00	0:10:00
	3	0:00:45	0:01:30	0:03:00	0:04:30	0:06:00	0:09:00	0:12:00	0:15:00
	4	0:01:00	0:02:00	0:04:00	0:06:00	0:08:00	0:12:00	0:16:00	0:20:00
Total Number of Share Outs	5	0:01:15	0:02:30	0:05:00	0:07:30	0:10:00	0:15:00	0:20:00	0:25:00
	6	0:01:30	0:03:00	0:06:00	0:09:00	0:12:00	0:18:00	0:24:00	0:30:00
	7	0:01:45	0:03:30	0:07:00	0:10:30	0:14:00	0:21:00	0:28:00	0:35:00
	8	0:02:00	0:04:00	0:08:00	0:12:00	0:16:00	0:24:00	0:32:00	0:40:00
	9	0:02:15	0:04:30	0:09:00	0:13:30	0:18:00	0:27:00	0:36:00	0:45:00
	10	0:02:30	0:05:00	0:10:00	0:15:00	0:20:00	0:30:00	0:40:00	0:50:00
	12	0:03:00	0:06:00	0:12:00	0:18:00	0:24:00	0:36:00	0:48:00	1:00:00
	16	0:04:00	0:08:00	0:16:00	0:24:00	0:32:00	0:48:00	1:04:00	1:20:00
	20	0:05:00	0:10:00	0:20:00	0:30:00	0:40:00	1:00:00	1:20:00	1:40:00
	24	0:06:00	0:12:00	0:24:00	0:36:00	0:48:00	0:12:00	1:36:00	2:00:00
	30	0:07:30	0:15:00	0:30:00	0:45:00	1:00:00	1:30:00	2:00:00	2:30:00

Less Than 10 Minutes   10-15 Minutes   15-20 Minutes   20-30 Minutes   Over 30 Minutes

Remember that if you break the participants into subgroups for an activity, you may might need one share out per group.

If groups generate multiple artifacts, have each team choose one to share with the room, or just have the groups share with the people in their work group simultaneously.

Don't forget to add a buffer to account for the time it takes to start and end the share outs, as well as time for switching between participants.

Below we see two time estimates for how long it will take 6 people to share for 2 minutes. The first one only assumes the time it will take for each share. The second one is a little more realistic, allowing a minute up front for the first person to get ready, 30 seconds in between each person to allow for switching presenters, and 5 minutes at the end for reflection.

TRANSITIONING TO ONLINE

But...I like sticky notes. Being together is faster, and we get more done.

"Of course, co-location is still a highly effective way of working, but this scenario is increasingly unrealistic and also less desired. In a world where we mostly work on computer screens all day, we have to ask ourselves why we accept long commutes and costly real estate and infrastructure, just to sit in the same location every day with our colleagues. Effective remote collaboration can help us embrace a world where the locations of individuals no longer matter." **Bianka McGovern**, VP User Experience Goldman Sachs

We often hear pushback when we encourage teams to improve their remote work chops. We empathize. A face-to-face workshop is easier to plan, easier to control and we already have solid skills to run them. But how do you include remote participants?

Pointing webcams at whiteboards is torture. And what happens when you leave the room? It all goes away if you don't transcribe it (time consuming) or take photos (hard to read). Even collocated team members travel, so how do you keep momentum going no matter where anyone on the team is at any time? Remote work is on the rise. The sooner you're proficient with remote working, the sooner you'll benefit from digital-first flexibility.

Don't get caught without a plan. Here are five small steps you can take now to merge onsite and remote content:

SHARE PHOTOS IN REAL-TIME
Snap pics of sketches, whiteboards, and prototypes during the workshop, and add them to an online whiteboard. Prompt remote participants to add content around the photo.

BREAK-OUT BY LOCATION
Create ways for in-person groups and remote break-out groups to work independently. Co-located teams work face-to-face while remote participants interact on a different channel.

END SESSIONS DIGITALLY
Conclude your in-person collaboration session with an all-digital exercise. This helps keep the momentum going between in-person interactions.

TRANSCRIBE AS YOU GO

Enlist the help of others to capture workshop content digitally in real time. Involve remote participants and save the extra step of transcription.

TRY DIGITAL-FIRST

While going all digital from the beginning gets away from the tactile nature of sticky notes and paper, there are benefits to fully digital collaboration.

"Oh, alright. I'll try digital-first. How do I get started?"

First, congratulate yourself on making a wise decision. In all seriousness, it takes perseverance to overcome the cultural inertia that desires things to stay as they are, or return to some fading vision of former glory.

We've assembled the material in the balance of this book to help you on your journey:

- Find inspiration from the case studies in the next section.
- Broaden your perception of facilitation as you read the workshop craft section.
- Utilize the checklists at the back of the book to help you plan your next workshop.
- Post our "Principles of Remote Facilitation" where you can see it!

ALTHOUGH THE PROCESS IS COMPLEX,

the transition from face-to-face participation to online collaboration is achievable if virtual teams have access to the necessary information, reliable technology and adequate tools, and work processes set up.

LAILA VON ALVENSLEBEN / Collaboration Coach & Remote Work Mentor

As part of Laila's master's thesis at Hyper Island she did some of the earliest and most complete research on remote design thinking. Check it out here: medium.com/remote-design-thinking

CASE
STUDIES

CASE STUDY: INTUIT
SERVICE DESIGN AT SCALE

As a global organization, Intuit was faced with reconciling its service strategy between product teams in the US and customer support teams in the Philippines. To find solutions together, the dispersed group held a remote workshop.

Principal Experience Designer, **Erik Flowers**, created a service blueprint in MURAL. Team members could access the blueprint using their own devices. Video conferencing and plenty of screens created the environment for fluid interaction.

Together, they were able to uncover critical issues in the customer experience as well as ideas to improve the customer's journey.

Collaborating digitally enabled the global team to participate on equal footing. There was also no need to transcribe paper-based content, saving hours of wasted time. And best of all, the team began iterating immediately after the workshop to resolve service gaps: they just picked up digitally where they left off.

**BEING DIGITAL AND
CLOUD-BASED**
allows you to scale methods across
the enterprise.

When everyone can see their role and
place in the experience, they are more
engaged and can participate in more
meaningful ways.

ERIK FLOWERS / Principal Experience Designer, Intuit

SERVICE DESIGN SNAPSHOT

TEAM CONFIGURATION
Split team

METHOD USED
Service Blueprinting

NUMBER OF PARTICIPANTS
10

TOOLS INVOLVED
- MURAL
- Zoom Video Conferencing
- Laptops, iPads
- Microsoft Surface Hub

TIME ZONES CROSSED
10

TIME SPENT TRANSCRIBING
0 Minutes

TRAVEL EXPENSES
$0

TIME TO FIND CORE ISSUES
2 Hours

CASE STUDY: TRELLO
DIGITAL REMOTE DESIGN SPRINTS

As a lead product designer at Trello, now part of Atlassian, **Chris Kimbell** works with product managers, designers, developers and marketers all over the world. Their challenge is to run effective remote workshops.

Using a wide range of tools, the design team is able to hold regular design sprints. Virtual workspaces let them share ideas quickly, diagram customer journeys and distribute hi-res assets for asynchronous use later.

Having a clear digitally-defined workspace also helps them attract and retain high-caliber talent. The design team at Trello also strives to simulate casual, spontaneous conversations that take place in person.

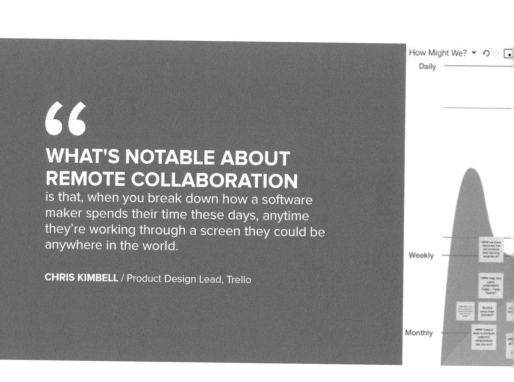

> **"**
> ## WHAT'S NOTABLE ABOUT
> ## REMOTE COLLABORATION
> is that, when you break down how a software maker spends their time these days, anytime they're working through a screen they could be anywhere in the world.
>
> **CHRIS KIMBELL** / Product Design Lead, Trello

DESIGN SPRINT SNAPSHOT

TEAM CONFIGURATION
All remote

METHOD USED
Multi-day design sprints

NUMBER OF PARTICIPANTS
5-10

TOOLS INVOLVED

- MURAL
- Trello
- Zoom
- Confluence
- Invision
- Figma
- Stride

TOTAL DURATION
2-3 Days

TIME SPENT TRANSCRIBING
0 Minutes

TRAVEL EXPENSES
$0

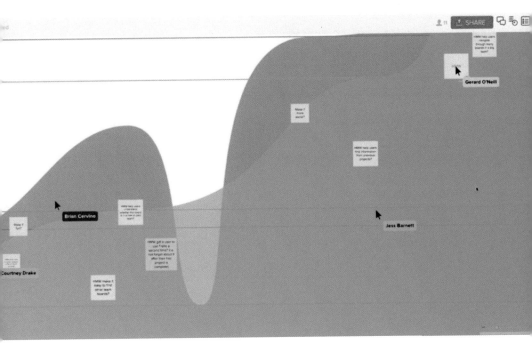

CASE STUDY: IBM
REMOTE DESIGN THINKING WORKSHOPS

Design thinking is part of IBM's culture, but with nearly 400,000 employees around the world, conducting design workshops proves difficult.

No one knows this better than **Jordan Shade** and **Eric Morrow**, design facilitators at IBM. To scale across the organization, they've translated their design thinking curriculum into remote-friendly workshops.

One key is to replicate aspects of a physical workshop, such as creating parking lots, rules of engagement, and agendas. They also recommend to plan for lots of silent activities, followed by group discussion.

Timing is key as well. Eric and Jordan plan short 10 minute (or less) exercises and limit overall workshop length to about 2 hours.

In the end, they're able to effectively engage teams around the world in design thinking workshops.

**OVERALL,
KEEP IT SHORT.**

During a live session there are plenty of activities that keep people engaged, including breaks and social activities. Online, it's all replaced by work. That's more exhausting mentally.

ERIC MORROW / Design Facilitator, IBM

WORKSHOP SNAPSHOT

TEAM CONFIGURATION
Mostly hybrid / All-remote

METHOD USED
Empathy Maps, Storyboards,
Lean Business Model Canvas

NUMBER OF PARTICIPANTS
Varies: small to large groups

TOOLS INVOLVED
- MURAL
- Zoom Video Conferencing
- Instant Messaging

TOTAL DURATION
2 hours per session

TIME SPENT TRANSCRIBING
0 Minutes

TRAVEL EXPENSES
$0

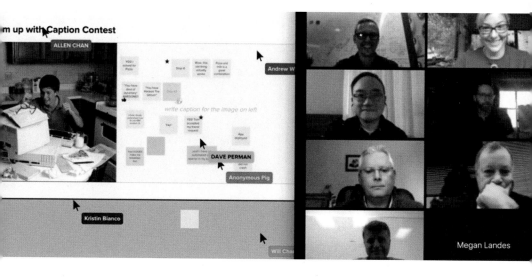

PART II
DIGITAL-FIRST PRACTICE

Facilitating remote workshops takes practice and confidence. Beyond the technologies and tools, it requires fresh approaches to traditional methods.

The good news is that you're not starting over from scratch. It's important to leverage existing facilitation skills you've mastered and bring those insights into each new remote workshop you design. As you prepare your favorite methods for remote-readiness, be mindful of the following:

MEANINGFUL SPACE Create boundaries, communicate the rules.
- Define where content is to be added.
- Consider how artifacts might move from one activity to the next.
- Use timeboxing to create a useful sense of urgency.

OPENING & CLOSING Kick off each activity, bring them to a close.
- Write a concise brief for each method.
- Ask for clarifying questions before you begin.
- Include time to reflect before the next exercise begins.

INPUTS & OUTPUTS Connect one activity to the next.
- Identify what's required to start and end each activity.
- Consider how much content will be generated.
- Include smaller, bridging activities to tidy up data for the next step.

FLOW Create an arc of experiences, from beginning to middle to end.
- Prepare and practice beforehand so you can be present during the event.
- Take ownership. Each group relies on you to guide them through the material.
- Be flexible. The unexpected happens. Enlist help, improvise and stay positive.

BE REMOTE-READY Prepare to execute methods remotely.
- Know the tools and test each method until confident.
- Get help running sessions so you can focus on facilitation, not troubleshooting.
- Share photos of any physical artifacts as the workshop progresses.

Leverage experience with in-person workshops to facilitate remote sessions. Some techniques will be limited (e.g., role playing remotely, or co-creating physical mockups), but be creative, leverage new technologies and take advantage of the benefits (e.g., pre-work, multitasking, and reducing transcription at the end).

We've all experienced the silence. No one wants to raise a hand. Participants avoid eye contact and clearly wish they were anywhere but where they are.

They don't feel their voices count, that they are supported by their peers or anything useful will come from this workshop.

According to Gallup, only 30% of workers agree strongly their opinions count. **Howard B. Esbin, PhD*** and CEO of Playprelude.com reminds us, **"When we don't speak up, it's mainly due to fear of failure, ridicule, and embarrassment. This is a great barrier to productivity, creativity and well-being."**

Even if you have a room of people willing to participate, they are not likely to have confidence in their ability to use new tools, use new methodologies or sketch ideas well enough to share with others. **"Find a safe and fun way to introduce users to the tools, for instance, with a quick warm-up exercise"** suggests **Holly Noto****, **"Help them gain confidence with the functionality and excitement for using the tools."**

Here are a few things you can do to generate trust and build confidence in your workshops:

TALK ABOUT IT Make "Safety and Confidence" part of the agenda.
- Tell them this is a safe place. Assure them they have the skills required.
- Include a short warm-up activity that helps people learn about each other.
- Invite a brief discussion about concerns that might block open participation.

FACILITATE IT Model the behaviors you'd like to see from the group.
- Make room for quiet voices. Reassure reluctant, shy participants.
- Use anonymous voting and individual work alongside group activities.
- Keep control of the conversation. Don't be afraid to quiet dominant voices.

*Howard is a co-creator of the Prelude Suite, an online experiential learning platform for virtual teams that helps accelerate trust through a facilitated process of self-understanding, self-expression, dialogue, and co-creation.

**Holly Noto, Consultant with XPLANE, is a change agent, helping teams and companies transform into modern, agile business through design thinking and visualization.

There are as many ways to assemble workshops as there are challenges to be solved.

While we can't address every potentiality in this book, we can share a typical example of a multi-day remote workshop. We'll provide commentary to unpack what's going on and that might help you riff off of it to design what you need.

The agenda below is for a workshop designed to run on two separate days within one week. It includes pre-work, as well as self-directed activity to be completed between the two real-time collaboration sessions.

SAMPLE WORKSHOP AGENDA DAY 1

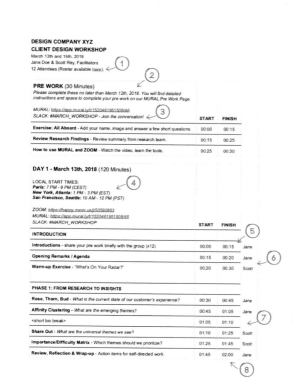

1. Link to a separate roster, that might change over time.

2. Include pre-work in the agenda. Set a due date.

3. Consider a dedicated channel where attendees can support each other.

4. List start times in local timezones to minimize confusion.

5. Show duration, not specific times when working across different time zones.

6. Split the work between two facilitators when possible.

7. Include a short break in longer sessions. Tack it to the end of an activity so people can choose to break or keep working.

8. Always allow time at the end for reflection and assigning action items.

Use the time in between the two real-time sessions for attendees to work independently. This allows the second session to be a little shorter but remain engaging and productive by focusing the time together on evaluation, critique and iteration of ideas.

SAMPLE WORKSHOP AGENDA DAY 2

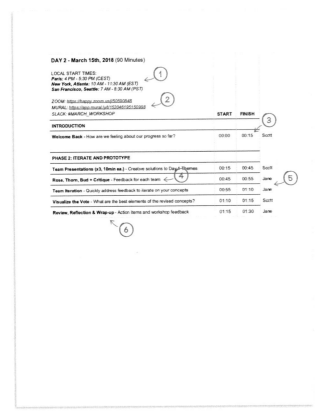

1. Vary the start times so one team is not always forced to participate outside of normal business hours.

2. Always include links to relevant tools, meeting links, and collaboration documents.

3. Allow time for attendees to warm up to the topic again. Even if there's some uncomfortable silence, give it time. Ask simple questions like, "Who learned something new since our last session?"

4. Remember to think through the time it will take for share-outs. Stick to your schedule with an audible timer.

5. If two methods flow together, it's good to keep the same facilitator for both.

6. Leave time to conclude as a group, and always request feedback on the workshop.

REMOTE-FRIENDLY METHODS

Workshops work best when they meet participants where they are, then guide them through a sequence of activities that comes to a clear conclusion with actions.

It might be helpful to think about this journey by its shape:

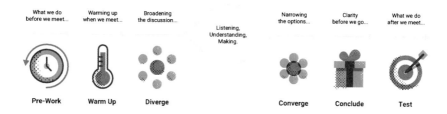

The following, remote-friendly methods are arranged in an order that follows this shape. These are by no means the only methods that work remotely, nor should you limit yourself to this set. They are merely examples of methods we've used with success arranged in the order in which you might consider using them to complete a "well-shaped workshop."

STEP	METHOD	OBJECTIVE
Pre-Work	• All Aboard	• Engage & Inform
Warm Up	• Me, In Images	• Introductions
Diverge	• Interviewing • What's On Your Radar? • Creative Matrix	• Research • Aligning • Generating
Converge	• Affinity Clustering • Visualize The Vote • Importance/Difficulty Matrix	• Pattern Finding • Taking Temperature • Prioritization
Conclude	• Design Studio	• Create & Iterate
Test	• Think Aloud Testing	• Testing

⏱ ENGAGE & INFORM

Get your workshop participants engaged before the workshop. Share helpful information and get hands-on time with the tools in advance.

METHOD: ALL ABOARD

Your workshop train is about to leave the station. Use this method to get everyone onboard.

TIME 10 MINUTES (individual pre-work)
- 30-90 seconds per participant

PARTICIPANTS 2-25

SETUP
- Create a shared mural or document that everyone can access prior to the workshop
- Define a space for each person to add their name and a photo
- Include a short poll or a few questions around their expectations for the workshop
- Add links to resources they should review before the workshop—like user research or tutorials for the tools you'll be using

MURAL EXAMPLE SCREENSHOT

ALL ABOARD

BEFORE THE WORKSHOP

STEP 1 ADD NAME AND PHOTO

Have each person claim a location to add their photo and name. Complete the first instance as an example.

STEP 2 ANSWER THE QUESTIONS

Provide a mix of serious and playful questions. Responses help you discover possible alignment issues between your goals and their expectations, but it's also an opportunity to learn about each other. Suggest creative ways to answer—with images, uploading a sketch or in the form of a haiku.

STEP 3 REVIEW THE LINKS

Remind participants of any required reading/viewing prior to the session.

AT THE WORKSHOP

STEP 4 SHARE OUT

Screen share the document. Welcome participants and start by reading your own entry. Keep it brief to model the expected length for the group. If 25 people take 2 minutes each, that's nearly an hour. Set a timer with an audible alarm so everyone knows when their time is up. Make the alarm a humorous sound, like a duck quacking, to lighten up the interaction.

VARIATION FOR REGULAR MEETINGS

If participants know each other, skip the name/photo and substitute with other topics, e.g., share recent user research findings, links to competitive products or relevant user metrics. Or make it personal, like a recent trip or relevant industry topic or news event to share with the team.

*Email **marketing@mural.co** for access to this activity template.

INTRODUCTIONS

Remote teams have few opportunities to get to know each other. Taking time to create a rapport among your participants will make collaboration smoother.

METHOD: ME, IN IMAGES

Making personal connections when working remotely is tough. Use images to get to know more about each other.

TIME 15-30 MINUTES

PARTICIPANTS 3-10

SETUP

- Use the "Team Kickoff Template" in MURAL for this exercise
- Invite your team to both the meeting and the mural in advance

MURAL EXAMPLE SCREENSHOT

ME, IN IMAGES

STEP 1 DESCRIBE YOURSELF IN IMAGES (2-3 MIN)

Do a web search for images that reflect your interests, hobbies and personality. Copy and paste 2-3 images into an area in the mural. Or, take a photo of your current workspace or outside your window to add. You can also ask participants to find a photo of their doppelganger. Be creative in what you require them to do. Set a timer for this part of the exercise.

STEP 2 SHARE YOUR IMAGES

Go around the group one by one and have each person describe the images they selected. Make sure they turn their webcams on, or if co-located in a room, have each person move close to the camera as they speak. Gestures and facial expressions make a difference in building a connection with remote teams. For Hybrid teams, alternate between in-room participants and remote participants to establish turn-taking norms between the two groups. Start with yourself, and model the type of empathetic language you'd like during the workshop in this early exercise.

PRO TIP

Try the "follow me" feature in MURAL for this to ensure everyone is looking at the same set of images.

Me, In Images is a favorite method of the MURAL team. We've used it successfully for demos and trainings in dozens of workshops.

*Email **marketing@mural.co** for access to this activity template.

 RESEARCH

Successful designs are fed with continual investigation. Get outside your own opinions and on a productive path with research.

METHOD: INTERVIEWING

You have two ears and one mouth. Use them in that ratio when conducting interviews.

TIME 15-30 MINUTES

PARTICIPANTS 3 PER GROUPING (1 interviewer, 1 note taker, 1 interviewee)

SETUP

- Identify an area of inquiry related to your project
- Identify stakeholders you can talk to
- Prepare your questions
- Schedule a time to connect

MURAL EXAMPLE SCREENSHOT

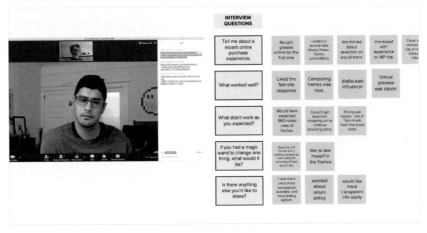

INTERVIEWING

DURING THE INTERVIEW
STEP 1 INTRODUCE YOURSELF
Use conference call software to connect with your participant with the webcams on. Say hello and share the purpose for the interview. Ask if it's okay to record the session.

STEP 2: ASK YOUR QUESTIONS
Start with simple questions and ask, "Can you say more?", to draw out details.

STEP 3 TAKE NOTES
Create a shared document to capture notes from the interview. If it's too hard to keep in up real-time, create a shorthand that you can expand on later. Invite others listening to the call to contribute as well.

STEP 4 SAY THANK YOU
Politeness counts and leaves the door open to follow up again if needed. Ask if the person would be willing to participate in an interview again.

AFTER THE INTERVIEW
STEP 5 CAPTURE YOUR OBSERVATIONS
Capture individual observations to individual notes in a shared digital workspace like MURAL. Share a link to any audio, video or notes with your team. Plan to invest as much time processing your notes as it took to conduct the interview.

GENERAL INTERVIEWING TIPS
- Create rapport with nodding and agreement (e.g., "Yes, I see how that's frustrating")
- Avoid yes-or-no questions to keep participants talking
- Dig deep and follow interesting thoughts (e.g., "Say more about...")
- Minimize distractions and avoid interruptions
- Use pauses to give the interviewee a chance to think and respond

For more on interviewing, we recommend the book, "Interviewing Users" by MURAL friend **Steve Portigal**.

*Email **marketing@mural.co** for access to this activity template.

⚙️ ALIGNING

Never assume your participants share a point of view on anything. Now is the time to surface the group's assumptions, priorities, goals and breaking news.

METHOD: WHAT'S ON YOUR RADAR

The sooner you identify an obstacle, the better your chance of correcting your course.

TIME 30 MINUTES

PARTICIPANTS 3-10

SETUP

- Create a shared mural or document with a "Bull's-eye" framework
- Label the innermost circle "Primary," the middle circle "Secondary" and the outer circle "Tertiary"
- Divide the circle into 4-8 quadrants like a pizza
- Label each sector to focus discussion around known topics, leaving 1-2 blank

MURAL EXAMPLE SCREENSHOT (LUMA Framework)

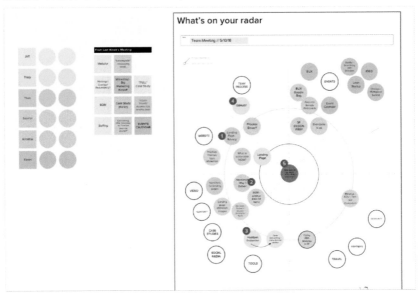

WHAT'S ON YOUR RADAR

STEP 1 INTERNAL AUDIT (3 MIN)

Ask participants to work quietly and create a note for each issue that is top of mind. Set a timer for this part of the activity and remind participants how much time is left with one minute to go.

STEP 2 SHARE OUT (1 MIN PER PERSON)

Go around the group and allow people to place their notes, one at a time, onto the primary, secondary or tertiary orbit of the appropriate slice. The more urgent the issue, the closer it should be to the center of the diagram. Use the list of participants on the conference software to include everyone or have the last person call on the next one to share.

STEP 3 CLARIFYING QUESTIONS & NEGOTIATIONS (4 MIN)

As they are placed, the group should ask questions if they are not clear on the issue. As more issues are placed, negotiate "primary" issues that might need to become "secondary" or "tertiary."

STEP 4 DISCUSS, TABLE, TAKE OFFLINE (5 MIN)

As a group, determine which topics to discuss, table or postpone for another meeting.

*Email **marketing@mural.co** for access to this activity template.

⁛ GENERATING

None of us is as creative as all of us. Group collaboration has the potential to open the creative floodgates, if facilitated correctly with the right method.

METHOD: CREATIVE MATRIX

Creative alchemy from asking what happens at the intersection of human needs and provocative ideas. This is brainstorming, but better. Use this to generate creative ideas to be worked on in another activity.

TIME 45 MINUTES

PARTICIPANTS 5-20

SETUP
- Create a shared mural or document that includes a 4x4 grid where notes can be placed by team members
- You will need a separate grid for each group of 4-6 participants
- Label each column header with a challenge statement, customer journey moment or relevant persona
- Label each row header with a suggestion, trend or relevant emerging technology to evoke creative ideas

MURAL EXAMPLE SCREENSHOT (LUMA Framework)

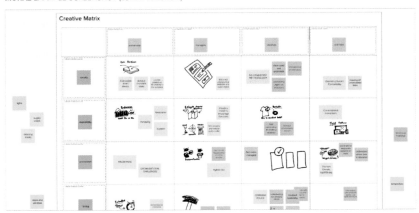

CREATIVE MATRIX

STEP 1 ORIENTATION (5 MIN)

Share your screen and walk participants through the matrix. Explain each column and row header. Mention that this is a competition, and the team that generates the most ideas will win. Also inform everyone that this is a silent activity. Talking gets in the way of adding lots of ideas. Clarify any questions before you begin.

STEP 2 ORGANIZE SUB-GROUPS (1 MIN)

Consider the participants' locations. If some are co-located it's good to let them work together and organize the other remote people into other sub-groups.

STEP 3 GO! (10 MIN)

Remind the groups to work silently as they consider each intersection and generate a note for each idea they have. Time this part and make sure people stop when the time is up. Play background music for an extra touch since this is a longer segment.

STEP 4 STOP! COUNT UP TOTALS (2 MIN)

Ask each group to count their notes and share the total. The group with the most notes "wins." The real winner is the group, and you can prove it by telling them how many ideas were generated in just 10 minutes!

STEP 5 REFLECT (10 MIN)

Ask each team to pick 1-2 ideas to share with all the attendees and discuss. See our guide to timing on page 23. Remember that if you have five groups and each takes 5 minutes to read out, that's 25 minutes.

Creative matrix is a favorite technique by our friends at **LUMA Institute**.

*Email **marketing@mural.co** for access to this activity template.

❀ PATTERN FINDING

At some point, the group will need to make sense of all the information they have gathered through research, or generated through an activity. Use a sorting method to find the dominant themes.

METHOD: AFFINITY CLUSTERING

When you sort by similarity, you can learn as much about your fellow teammates' point of view as you can about the information itself.

TIME 30 MINUTES

PARTICIPANTS GROUPS OF 3-5

SETUP

- Create a shared mural or document that allows free movement of individual notes
- Identify a collection of content that needs to be better understood
- This might be from interviews, survey results, or even customer feature requests
- Create individual notes for each item

MURAL EXAMPLE SCREENSHOT

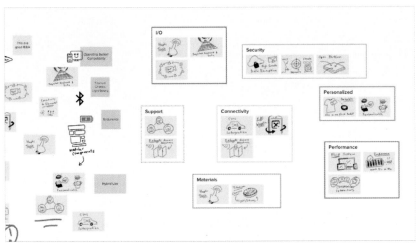

AFFINITY CLUSTERING

STEP 1 SILENT SORTING (5 MIN)
Working quietly as a group, have individuals move notes into clusters based on perceived similarity. Set a timer and add time as needed, e.g., in 1-2 minute increments. It's better to underestimate the time you'll need and add more than to overestimate.

STEP 2 VERBALIZE OR LABEL (10 MIN)
Have members of the group describe the clusters that have emerged. Provide a label for each group as you go.

STEP 3 REFINE CLUSTERS (10 MIN)
Have the group review large clusters. See if they contain multiple, distinct concepts that might be better as separate clusters.

STEP 4 SHOW RELATIONSHIPS (5 MIN)
Use lines, arrows or other visuals to highlight the interaction or dependency between clusters.

PRO TIP
With larger collections of content, pre-cluster your content before inviting others to work with it. Hundreds of notes from a dozen or more interviews looks daunting for any team asked to make sense of it in its raw form. Be careful not to bias them too much. Look for logical pre-bucketing you can do, such as loosely grouping content around the questions you asked. Creating a few pre-clustered categories makes the interaction run more smoothly. (Hat tip to **Stefanie Owens** from O'Reilly for this recommendation.)

*Email **marketing@mural.co** for access to this activity template.

✻ TAKING TEMPERATURE

It's wise to check in as a group throughout the workshop. Uncover hidden issues and divided opinion when you still have time to do something about it. Consider voting to set the context for further discussion, instead of wielding it to force a decision moments before the workshop ends.

METHOD: VISUALIZE THE VOTE

Take a quick poll to reveal the preferences and opinions of the group.

TIME 10 MINUTES

PARTICIPANTS 3-30

SETUP
- Identify the subject for the polling activity
- Decide if there will be one or more factors to vote upon
- Determine how many votes each person is allowed per factor

MURAL EXAMPLE SCREENSHOT

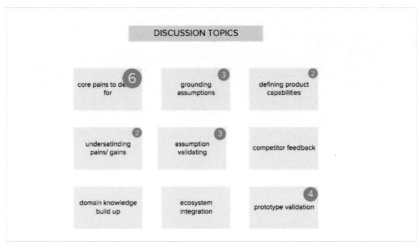

VISUALIZE THE VOTE

STEP 1 PREPARE THE VOTERS

Clearly describe what preference their vote indicates. Are they allowed to vote for more than one thing? Can they vote on their own items? You decide.

STEP 2 INITIATE THE VOTE

To avoid bias, have everyone consider how they will vote first, then have everyone cast their vote at the same instant. For instance, use a shared chat to type in voting results individually, but don't hit enter until everyone has finished typing. Or, use MURAL's integrated voting feature.

STEP 3 DISCUSS THE RESULTS

Call out results for each factor under consideration. Examine the outliers. Have people share why they chose or rejected certain items.

*Email **marketing@mural.co** for access to this activity template.

✿ PRIORITIZING

While all ideas may have merit, there comes a time when the group needs to decide which ones will be taken forward, and which ones are left for another time.

METHOD: IMPORTANCE/DIFFICULTY MATRIX

Reach agreement on the relative impact of the ideas before discussing how much effort it will take to accomplish each one.

TIME 40 MINUTES

PARTICIPANTS GROUPS OF 2-5

SETUP
- Create a shared mural or document where notes can be arranged within a 2x2 grid
- Each group will require its own grid
- Label the horizontal axis "Importance," or "Impact"
- Label the vertical axis "Difficulty," "Cost" or "Effort"
- Schedule one or more video conferences as needed for breakout groups

MURAL EXAMPLE SCREENSHOT (LUMA Framework)

IMPORTANCE/DIFFICULTY MATRIX

STEP 1 EXPLAIN ACTIVITY TO EVERYONE (5 MIN)

It's important for everyone to understand that there are three distinct steps to this method, and they must be done step by step to be effective. Choose 6-12 items that require prioritization and make a note for each one. Sort horizontally by importance. Force the distribution, there are no ties. Sort vertically (maintaining horizontal order) by difficulty. Again, force distribution. Let them know a final step will be explained later. Share your screen as you talk through this, being sure to invite questions until everyone in clear on the brief.

STEP 2 ORGANIZE SUB-GROUPS (2 MIN)

Consider the participants' locations. If some are co-located it's good to let them work together and organize the other remote people into other sub-groups. Based on the video conference tool you use, it may be necessary to schedule and share multiple meetings to accommodate each group. We highly recommend tools like Zoom that have breakout room functionality built-in.

STEP 3 TEAMS BEGIN. YOU FACILITATE (15 MIN)

Move between conference lines listening to each group's progress. Based on the tips below, remind teams of the protocol and keep them on track. Time this segment and give everyone a 2-minute warning.

STEP 4 REGROUP FOR THE FINAL STEPS (5 MIN)

Demonstrate labeling the quadrants as follows: Upper-left, "LUXURY"; Upper-right, "STRATEGIC"; Lower-left, "Low-hanging Fruit" and Lower-right, "High ROI." Then draw two diagonal lines that divide the 2x2 grid into three equal areas. Lower-right is "Do this First." The center area that goes from lower-left to upper-right is "Do this Second." The third area that is in the upper-left is "Do this Third." Allow each team a moment to complete these additions.

STEP 5 DISCUSS (10 MIN)

Share your screen and facilitate a brief share out from each group. Display each team's end result and have them nominate someone to present their results to the other teams.

*Email **marketing@mural.co** for access to this activity template.

CREATING & ITERATING

After defining the right problem to solve, use a chain of activities to solve the problem right.

METHOD: DESIGN STUDIO

Harness group imagination to quickly iterate and improve ideas.

TIME 30-90 MINUTES

PARTICIPANTS 2-10

SETUP
- Start with the "Design Studio Template" in MURAL
- Add the challenge statement to the area indicated for round 1
- Invite the group to the document and begin

MURAL EXAMPLE SCREENSHOT

DESIGN STUDIO

STEP 1 ASSIGN WORKING LANES (1 MIN)
Instruct each person to find a row on the table and place their name and photo to the left.

STEP 2 BRAINSTORM (2 MIN)
Instruct each person to think of as many unique solutions to the challenge as they can, adding a note for each in the first column of their row. Set a timer for this part of the activity.

STEP 3 SKETCH (10 MIN)
Instruct each person to pick their favorite idea and sketch it out in the second column of their row. If they are sketching on paper, have them take a picture and upload it. Time this segment and give everyone a 2-minute warning.

STEP 4 SHARE (2-5 MIN PER PERSON)
Each person presents a concept sketch and the feedback is captured in the third column. Be sure to highlight strong aspects of the concepts that might provide superior solutions. Use webcams to see the person presenting as they talk through their sketch.

STEP 5 CONSOLIDATE (5 MIN)
Describe a single solution that combines the best elements from the group. Sketch the new, combined concept and agree on a direction as a group.

Iterate on the first concept or start a new design studio for this next challenge.

*Email **marketing@mural.co** for access to this activity template.

 TESTING

Resist the urge to wait until everything is perfect.
Get your concepts in front of people early and often.
The feedback you receive helps you eliminate errors
while refining the concept.

METHOD: THINK ALOUD TESTING

If you could only know what people are thinking as they interact
with your product. Oh, wait...you can! Share your sketch,
prototype or mock-up with someone and ask them to narrate
their experience as they go.

TIME 15-30 MINUTES

PARTICIPANTS 6-9

SETUP
- Identify what you will test and one or two key tasks
- Develop a mockup or prototype able to support participants interaction
- Identify one person to facilitate and one person to record observations of the participant.
- Prepare screen recording software or camera to capture the test

MURAL EXAMPLE SCREENSHOT

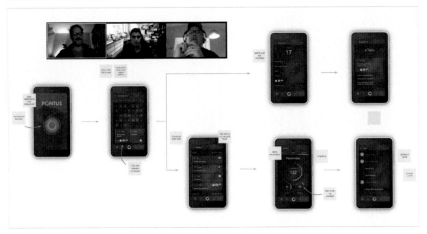

THINK ALOUD TESTING

DURING THE TEST
STEP 1 INTRODUCTIONS

Introduce the concept to the test participants. Explain their role in the simulation and ask if they have any questions. Remind them to verbalize what they are doing and thinking. Be sure to let them know there are no mistakes and no wrong answers.

STEP 2 OBSERVATION

Simulate use of the product or service with your prototype. Do not answer questions about the prototype or guide their actions. Observe their actions and record their narrative.

STEP 3 CLOSING

When they complete the simulation, thank them for their participation.

AFTER THE TEST
STEP 4 MODIFY PROTOCOL OR PROTOTYPE

Based on the first few testing experiences, modify the simulation or tweak the protocol, or both.

STEP 5 CONSOLIDATE NOTES

Look across the notes from your tests. Identify the elements that are working well and which ones risk failure for the experience. Share this with the product team.

*Email **marketing@mural.co** for access to this activity template.

CHECKLISTS & GUIDES

PREPARE

Step	Remote Recommendations	✓

MAP OUT LOGISTICS

Goals: Ensure team reaches objectives / Maximize participation from the right stakeholders / Optimize collaboration for different locations

Set Goals	Communicate explicit objectives to keep the remote groups on track. What do you want to get out of the workshop?
Select Participants	Groups of 10-25 people work best. Hands-on activities are difficult with larger groups. Include a mix of roles for diverse perspectives.
Determine How To Collaborate	Strategize for your team's remote situation. You will likely need a mix of tools that you should set up and test in advance.
Set Date, Time, Length	2 to 4-hour sessions work best. Schedule multiple segments if needed, and work asynchronously when possible. Be aware of time zones.
Schedule Location, Means	Reserve rooms and equipment for in-person participants. Schedule a video call and make sure remote participants join from in a quiet place.

DETERMINE METHODS

Goals: Foster creativity in the group / Create a smooth flow / Maximize engagement during the workshop

Select Activities	Choose activities to engage the group and reach your objectives. A 3-hour workshop might have 4-6 exercises (~30+ minutes each).
Customize, Modify Methods	Not every exercise will work "out of the box" in a remote setting. Adapt steps to work with the tools you'll have in a remote context.
Time Exercises, Activities	Set time limits to keep attention focused. Break up activities into short steps (1-5 mins each). Estimate low: you can always add more time if needed.
Create A Flow	Create an arc to the workshop. Visualize the overall flow for yourself and for others to see and follow along.
Plan Engagement	Keep the action going. Leverage multitasking and require participants to use different channels, e.g., switch from chat to video to a document and back.
Set Up Templates	Map out the spaces to work in documents or in MURAL. Number steps clearly for orientation. Give participants a sense of what's coming next.
Rehearse Exercises	Run through each step by yourself or with a co-facilitator to identify potential issues, e.g., the time needed per exercise, etc.

SET UP WORKSHOP

Goals: Increase likelihood of participation / Reduce risk of getting off track / Maximize collaboration time together

Create A Dashboard	Set up a central place online (e.g., in a mural) to both introduce the purpose of the workshop and summarize the outcomes. This serves as a home base for the team.
Invite Others	Invite participants and send reminders. Be clear about what's expected of them. Outline details of the team, tools and tasks.
Introduce Tools	Remote sessions slow down if just one person can't use the tools effectively. Ensure everyone has access, and include links and guides to learn in advance.
Assign Pre-Work	Get a head start with pre-work. Send a calendar invitation to remind people to complete it. Start a group chat about the workshop to get the ball rolling before you meet.
Hold A Pre-Session Call	Hold a short call to go over housekeeping items a few days in advance. Introduce everyone, review tools and introduce activities and goals.
Answer Follow Up Questions	Reach out to participants after you assign pre-work. Confirm their participation and answer any follow up questions.

RUN WORKSHOP

Step	Remote Recommendations	✓

ORIENT TEAM

Goals: Create a safe, creative environment / Ensure equal participation from everyone / Reduce the risk of getting off track

Kick Off Session	Join early and greet people as they come. Evaluate their setting and make adjustments, e.g., let someone know about background noise or troubleshoot access issues.
Make Introductions	If you haven't done so, make sure everyone is introduced. (See method "Me In Images"). Have them share personal details for better team building.
Onboard Participants	Go over the tools and have everyone use each application briefly to verify that they can collaborate. Distribute email addresses and chat handles to connect the group.
Warm Up	Get creative juices flowing with a warm-up exercise. Integrate the remote setting, e.g., have everyone share a photo of their workspace.

RUN ACTIVITIES

Goals: Maximize the effectiveness of each activity / Increase participation from the team / Ensure objectives are met

Explain Techniques	Over-communicate instructions of each activity and demonstrate exactly what is expected. Show what a completed exercise might look like.
Assign Roles	Don't leave roles to chance in remote settings. Designate co-facilitators, discussion leads, scribes and workshop producers in advance.
Work Individually	Favor exercises that can be done individually. Use mobile phones to take photos of sketches or flipcharts. Time each exercise, play music to fill the silence.
Work In Breakout Groups	Break-out groups are difficult with a single audio channel, but possible. Some software has a break-out feature (e.g., Zoom).
Discuss As A Group	Come back together and discuss your work. Take turns so everyone participates. Use webcams to enhance nonverbal communication.

CONCLUDE

Goals: Understand the workshop outcomes as a group / Increase the team's ability to make decisions / Keep the creative momentum going

Find Patterns	Cluster concepts to find common themes. Use a digital whiteboard to visualize your work.
Decide Together	Get team consensus using chat for quick polling. Or, set up a poll in advance or use MURAL's integrated voting feature.
Document What Happened	Capture content in shared documents and on digital whiteboards as its created. Designate scribes to ensure everything is documented.
Create An Action Plan	Assign owners to action items and create a preliminary project plan. Set up project management in advance to ensure follow up.
Assign Post-Work	Prepare action items and assign them at the end, e.g., further prioritization or secondary research (e.g., competitor comparisons). Also plan a follow-up call.
Reflect	Compare workshop outcomes to your goals and reflect on the workshop. Create a space in a mural or shared document for feedback or set up a quick survey.

FOLLOW UP

Step	Remote Recommendations	✓

SHARE RESULTS

Goals: Increase visibility of workshop output / Reduce the chance people don't follow up on action items / Maximize the impact of outcomes

Send A Summary	Send workshop artifacts to participants immediately afterwards. Update your workshop dashboard with the key results and feedback from the group.
Meet Again	Hold a short call afterwards to keep momentum. Schedule it before the workshop even begins. Reflect on the workshop and check progress.
Integrate Results	Integrate outputs into other documents. Take screenshots, export murals, and download documents to include in your final presentations.
Share Results With Others	Schedule a call to share results with stakeholders. Simulate the parts of the workshop and include them in a quick exercise (e.g., voting).
Gather Feedback	Make stakeholder presentations interactive. Have them prioritize content or evaluate roadmaps with a quick poll. Re-create part of the workshop for them to feel involved.
Manage Action Plan	Update your project plan with stakeholder feedback. Use team input for the next iteration and remote work session. Follow up with participants.

REFINE METHODS

Goals: Improve remote workshop skills / Establish best practices for your team / Maximize the reuse of materials

Reflect And Update	Evaluate the effectiveness of your methods and facilitation in a retrospective. Incorporate feedback from the team into how you'll run your next workshop.
Archive Work	Create copies of materials for future reference. Keep a consistent naming convention, and strive to increase their discoverability.
Reuse Materials	Create templates from your workshop for future use. Create a document or folder to maintain best practices. Create a case study to share with others.

Things will go wrong. Be prepared.

"Remote facilitation comes with a multitude of variables and challenges. Being able to prepare and plan for each potential variable is wise though not realistic. However, being able to pivot when something does not goes as planned, in a seamless and professional manner, can help lead to an undiscovered, potentially more successful outcome." **Jenny Price**, Designer, Facilitator and AIGA President's Council Chair.

TROUBLESHOOTING GUIDE

PROBLEM	DIAGNOSE
People are bored	Stop talking, ask a question. What prevents them from engaging? Are these the right participants? Is the timing awkward for their time zone?
People are distracted	Multi-tasking happens. Is it momentary or chronic? Can it be leveraged? Ask them to look up something for the group. Do people need a short break?
Timing doesn't work	Running overtime is very common. Can you safely omit an activity? Can you reduce the number of share outs? Can you break the agenda into two sessions?
Technology doesn't work	Find out how many are affected. Can someone take over troubleshooting? Can you shift the agenda order? Can you move to discussion and take notes?
Confused by exercise	How many are confused? Can someone help coach a small group? Do you need to start again with everyone? Can you make it simpler to complete?
Not showing up on time	Life happens. Was it unavoidable? Can they catch up at a break? Should the workshop start later? Can they contribute in advance or asynchronously?
Poor WIFI / No internet	How many are affected? Can you continue without those affected? Can you reschedule the session? Can you use alternate wifi access? (Cellular)
Nose and feedback	What type of audio problem is it? Diagnose an echo right away. Mute participants by default or manually. Call back in, sometimes that fixes the issue.